OUR BRAVE NEW WORLD

ANIKA SPEAKS

First published in Great Britain in 2020 by Anika Speaks

anika@anikaspeaks.com

Typesetting and layout: Anika Speaks

For all my children, in heaven and on earth

CONTENTS

FOREWORD

I have written poetry all my life, and with the lockdown of 2020, it actually inspired me to write even more. Each one is written with a positive message to give hope for a different life—one that is much more beautiful and glorious.

We all struggle at times, and nobody expected the need for a lockdown—we have not experienced a situation like this for over 100 years, the time of the Spanish flu. You might have imagined it would be ok and that everything would go back to normal. Well, you can never reclaim the old normal, but we can all learn to live in the new normal that emerges.

So I wrote these poems to reflect all of this and to give you a foretaste of Our Brave New World.

AUTHOR'S NOTE

Please believe me when I say
These are no idle words of mine
Each poem was birthed in its power
Its phrases carefully penned

This season's not like one before
This time has never been seen
With everybody in their house
Waiting for the word of freedom

Freedom to step out of doors
To get back to life again
It will never be the same life
As we'll discover then

We cannot tell what will come
Although know it will be different
The shape of our new world
Glitters from the distance

The future lies within our grasp
We can change the shape of millions
You do your part and I'll do mine
Together we'll make a difference

HOW DO WE TALK?

How do we talk in a myriad of ways?
How do we share when our voices seem silenced?
When all the world is screaming and shouting
And our whispering sound is lost in the shadows

You know just what you want to say
There always is an answer
The world is changing in our time
And we don't know what is coming

Our former life has gone away
The future will be different.
We need to share our thoughts with others
Give them just that glimpse of hope.

Hope is what the world needs now
A voice to give them that light
Changing what is now in darkness
Into a new and glorious day

The screaming now must be silenced
So that we can build tomorrow
The future is what lies before us
A world of difference to our eyes

Just listen for that tiny voice
The little words of comfort
That gives us hope the end is better
Than all we know right now

YOU COULD NOT HAVE KEPT THE WORLD SO QUIET

You could not have kept the world so quiet
For anything other than this
People are staying in their houses
Not venturing out of doors

The comparative silence of the streets
The emptiness at the doctor's
Really had it not been for this
The noise would have been deafening

And now the silence is the noise
As we stay within our doors
Trying to beat this awful virus
That has spread around the world

Time alone with family
Is what we have all night and day
There is no other option
Can't meet friends anywhere

But there is an escape you know
The world has gone online
Here you can meet other people
Respond to them in time

You can join the joys and sorrows
Of your friends on the internet
There is so much that can be discovered
In ways we didn't imagine

And people are doing different things
From what they've always done
Life has become a brand new place
And we've become part of it

SO TELL ME, WHAT DO YOU SEE?

So tell me, what do you see?
In the start and end of the day
Is it the promise of beginning
Or hope as it comes to its close?

Or do you just mark off the days
As something to be got through?
We're going through an unusual time.
How will we get to the end?

There's beauty in ending and starting
And everything in between
As we wait on the news before us
The end to all of our woes

But how can we be positive
When so many things are bad?
Take time to gather yourself
And assess everything you know

This may be where you want
Or you might find it differently
Are you hunting for the secret
That happiness comes from within?

Nobody gives you what you need
You must go out and seek it
I promise that it will come to you
With ending and beginning

Will it ever be easy?
Now that I cannot tell you
But there's one thing I know
That love is found in the heart

WHAT IS IT THAT MOVES YOU?

What is it that moves you?
What makes your heart sing?
What fills your days with laughter
And satisfies your very soul?

Days of pain and pleasure
But with sunlight peeping in
There is that silver lining
Or the gold at the end of a rainbow

Maybe not in the way you thought
Or the way you dreamed it would
But it will come to you
As you find that peace inside

For me it comes with writing
And seeing my home happy
I love to think of little things
And friends from far and near

Music also fills me with joy
As does gorgeous paper
I can see how it will be filled
With a pen that glides across

I don't like discord at all
It makes my heart so sad
I want to put the world to right
While sitting in my chair

But through the fire comes the gold
And everything worthwhile
So find the breath of life for you
And stay within its grasp

IT'S NOT EASY TO SEE THE BLESSINGS

It's not easy to see the blessings
That surround us every day
When life suddenly changes for us
And becomes a different one

How will we react to this
At the time it happens to us?
There is no manual for this life
Cause we all face things differently

But the blessings really are there
When most things seem hard to bear
It might be difficult to find them
But we must always try

What is good about this life?
Well, living is a blessing
But if you wish to be happy
Being positive is the key

Not in the sense of ignoring things
That you need to deal with now
But in the true sense of the word
Always bringing you joy

It's easy to look back and say
That things were different then.
Life is how it is today
And that's where we must find it

Blessings really should be counted
And be treasured also
For in times of weakness or sickness
They'll bring joy to you

So live your life with counted blessings
And make sure beauty remains
Remembering the good things
And point out what is there now

Your children will be thankful too
As they remember the beauty you shared
Finding joy in little things
And bringing light into their lives.

Blessings are simply everywhere
And you can choose to notice them
Fill your life with joy abounding
And pour into others too

HOW DO YOU THINK YOU WILL REACT?

How do you think you will react
When everything is open?
There'll be so many differences
But places seen will look the same

Look at the life we now are living
Every day inside the house
I must admit days look the same
Although each one is different

We are moving on you see
To what it is that lies ahead
I can't tell the shape it takes
The future's hidden to us

I know we know what we can do
And the things we shouldn't
Our freedom is now restricted
But there'll be a day it isn't

What's the first thing you want to do
When the ban is lifted from us?
I know there must be something
That makes you smile inside

The thing that touches you the most
Is one of those you'll do
When our lives are given back to us
And we can return to life

Life not as we knew it
But still a life, you'll see
Some things will be different
While others stay the same

Create a new life while you can
Say goodbye to the old ways
We have a chance to transform
The world while we're in limbo

ANXIETY

Anxiety comes so strong in the mind
What of all the people that are dead?
What about the ones who have survived?
What about those that are healthy and hearty?

We don't have much time any more
But then, we never did
It's just that right now it is obvious
When we're all in our houses alone

You miss the people you used to see
You don't have the same contact
Life has never been like this before
It's a pause before a new world start

But what will this new world be like?
Well that's for us to determine
We can recreate what went before
Or make a whole different life

So you can think of the new world to come
And not the one that has been
The world is going through massive change
And you're going along with it

What exactly will you change?
Does it bring you anxious thoughts?
What you decide needs to be done
A plan for emerging life again

Anxiety is a terrible beast
But you can turn things around
And if you need support
I know that you can find it

Support helps anxiety pass
And gives you strength to do things
Look at what you need to do
And what you need to do it

DO YOU NEED TO ALWAYS BE STRONG?

Do you need to always be strong
With never a tear in your eye?
Do you always have to stand up
As a strong and stable tree?

Strength doesn't come like this
It can be gentle and mild too
You can feel all the feelings you like
And still be there for others

Strong people aren't the ones who never crack
They feel just what they need to
Allowing each thought to take its place
And passing through their mind

Do they ever cry out for help?
Oh yes, they do so often
They recognise the signs
Before anything bad happens

Giving and receiving takes from you
Leaving you depleted and drained
Replenish and replace your strength
And it will be there for you

Strength comes from knowing when
The time has come to ask for help
So please don't sit there suffering
Find all of the help you need

Settle back and you will see
Strength comes from seeing
And putting things right as you go
So others can lean on you too

IN THE NIGHTS

In the nights of stillness
When all the world is quiet
What is it you think of
In the time that you're alone?

Do you wonder what will happen?
Or do you think about the past?
Is there something you forgot?
Things that need to be done?

What is it with you right now?
You think you're so alone
That nobody cares for you
Because no one is there

Do you know what's real?
Can you tell if it is false?
Do you want to share your life?
So you'll never be alone?

Finding someone who will care
Trusting them with who you are
And touch your heart in places
That you never knew were there

But will they even want you?
Is there something wrong with you?
Do you need to change your life?
So they will want to stay

Trusting again isn't easy
I know because I've done it
No matter what you think
There's always someone there

Maybe it's not who you thought
That happens to embrace you
You can learn to open up
And feel their love surround you

CHANGE

How do you cope with a drastic change
That's forced upon you so to speak?
To keep not only the world
But also you and yours safe

One person can make an impact
In many good ways or bad.
We have seen evidence of this
How one person makes a difference

So to stay at home you see
Is clearly what we have to do
There is no other way forward
To fight this spreading virus

All the world seems in lockdown
So many now are sick
But we need to remain healthy
And do the best we can

People that we thought important
Have turned out to not be so
The ones that we have needed
Are not the ones that we believed

So while some of us work away
The rest of us must stay
Coping with our life indoors
And fight the virus this way

SUDDEN CHANGE

So when a sudden change in life
Just hits you where you stand
It's wise to take a step back
And listen to what it's brought you

It may seem like an empty void
At first life could all be grey
But when you look around you'll see
The sunshine through the rain

The rainbow of hope can come to you
And make an impact as things stand
A ray of light from deep within
Can bring comfort in the darkness

If you cannot see the silver lining
Go ask someone you know
I'm sure they'll help you find it
It's not that far away

Yes, it can bring up problems
But there are solutions too
Each time a change comes to you
Find the good things in its wake

Sudden changes shatter hearts
Or fixes them with molten gold
Just remember when it comes to you
You find the blessing there too

A CHANGE

A change is being forced on us
One not many had been expecting
In fact many have been screaming
They don't want it to be this way

But it is and life cannot change
While this stalker covers the planet
Waiting to see who he may devour
As he wreaks havoc on our world

Being indoors isn't easy
Nobody ever finds it so
But it's something we have to do
If we all want to destroy this

Screaming in anger doesn't help
Nor does crying in a corner
It is what it is and so that's it
Gives us a chance to make a change

A change that could transform our life
The chance to make a difference
I wish that you could see it
The future that lies before you

Different roads you could follow
Go other directions, too
It doesn't matter where you go
As long as you are happy with it

DID YOU LOSE YOURSELF?

Did you lose yourself already?
Forget who you were meant to be
Did you find it was too much?
And so you grew a mask

Growing older the mask grew bigger
Covering the hidden spaces
Thinking that you could return
But it became much darker

Harder to find your true self
Which mask to wear today?
Who it was you were seeing
And soon these masks stayed

But how do you get rid of masks?
Something has to change
You need to realise what you're doing
And the price that you have paid

You'll never get the answer
Or even understand things
Changing your mindset isn't easy
But something needs to be done

So now you have to peel back layers
Like an onion shedding its skin
Yes, you will cry over some things
But don't worry, that's alright

Peel back each and every layer
Until you reach your true core
Find the truth that holds you
And live it each and every day

OUR LIVES REALLY AREN'T OVER

Our lives really aren't over
Just because we're in a holding state
But they are completely different
From everything we've ever known

The time has come for us to change
Our expectations now
We won't come out from our seclusion
The same as we went in

Life will be different yet again
From what we knew in the past
But we can make the changes needed
And bring about our brave new world

We don't know when our new existence
Will become a part of life
But there is one thing I know
We can prepare ourselves for it

The joy in life for us will be
The differences we bring
The sameness that we share
And celebrating them both

This is a chance for us to grow
And develop how we want
We can bring a brand new life
To our new world existence

I KNOW LIFE ISN'T WHAT YOU WANTED

I know life isn't what you wanted
You never thought this day would come
A time where you would live inside
Never seeing other people

Life can change so fast, you see
I wonder what will happen next
It will not go back to what it was
What will that difference be?

We know the way we react to things
Will bring changes to our lives
The decisions we make now
Change the future before us

Our children are now living a life
That we could never have dreamed of
Isolation all over the world
Has caused us to think differently

How can we adapt to this existence
And change what we have always done?
It's not an easy thing to do
Just what we have to achieve

We have discovered what's important
Developing our experiences
As we lived within our homes
We learnt what we need to know

TRANSITION

It's a time of great transition
During a period of vulnerability
Nobody is truly safe
As the virus grows and spreads

The face of the world will change
As we encounter the new beginnings
That come from struggles we have
Emerging from our cocoons

Stopping the world screaming
Isn't as easy as it sounds
We're facing new things
As our lives are remade in front of us

Things will seem the same but different Everything looks as it should be
But our lives are forever changed
Because a virus has run rampant

We will tell our children's children
Of the time when things went wrong
We had to stay shut up at home
Pausing to protect our lives

Only we can resolve this
Allow the changes to emerge
The flicker of hope remains within
As our lives pass before us

SOMETHING GOOD OUT OF THIS TRAGEDY

Can something good come out of this?
There is always a positive no matter what
A silver lining to every cloud
Changing usinto who we will become

Yes this is possible in our day and time
That transition contains transformation
Beauty in the new world to come
Born out of the sorrow of this time

Giving us time to find what's valuable
Leaving oh, so much behind
Finding out what is important
Guiding us to find what's right

Strangers too will give you help
Enabling you to restore your faith
In the people around you
And know that they are worthy

Trust will come to all of us
We will know just what to do
To help whenever we are able
Giving to others unselfishly

This gives you time now to reflect
And think of what you want
Looking to see what you can do
To help the lives of others

You don't know what this really means
Until you look for the answers
There's always something positive
To embrace, as we go through our day

GOLDEN OPPORTUNITY

Take this golden opportunity
Transform it to a good one
This time will never come again
In my lifetime or yours

Things aren't as they always were
We're starting a new existence
Our lives are now so different
Not something we expected

We could never have conceived
A life parked in just four walls
Only our homes the place to go
Elsewhere the doors are closed

Things have got so bad
Millions are shut inside
Nothing has been like it
In any other lifetime

We can change things now, you see?
Make our lives so differently
Plan out what we're going to do
When we open our doors again

These doors of opportunity
Will never come again
We must consider what we'll do
Ensure we make the most of it

Making changes as we discover
And find out what we're meant to do
There's never been a chance like this
To make some drastic changes

So take this golden opportunity
And use it not only for your good
But blessing to those around you
A treasure for your life

PURPOSE FOR LIVING

Do you feel there's a purpose for your living?
Do you ever wonder what you're here to do?
Do you think there must be a reason
Or you're not here at the right time?

Well I have discovered my meaning,
I know where my future will lead.
I am here at the season intended
To make a difference to others

The time is now for me to reach you
That moment when you read or hear
The words I'm sent to express
To help bring you peace and joy

There are people in need of you
That depend on what you do
Your purpose is a designed one
You're here at the right time

I don't know what is meant for you
Your life truly is your own
The people you make contact with
Also need what you bring to them

Please don't feel your life is worthless
I'm here to say that it's not
You bring something to each person
That enters your sphere

So take your life and its meaning
Hold fast to the ideas you have
There always is a reason
For your presence here on earth

Please don't just dismiss yourself
You have good qualities too
An excellence only you can give
In the work you're here to do

Discover your life's meaning
And live within its essence
Because somewhere within it
You can touch the depth of others

Touching the lives of others
Is something we can aspire to
Because making a difference to them
Makes changes within you

JUST KEEP SWIMMING

Do you know what I heard today?
That we must just keep swimming
It sounds so easy when you say it
But so much harder to do

How are you going to just keep swimming?
This isn't just for certain days
One thing we have to recognise
We're fighting wherever we are

But there isn't a battle, so you say
This isn't World War One!
No but there is similarity
To the Spanish flu that followed

We have never had to stay
For prolonged times inside
But we must fight this illness
By doing what is right

Staying inside is the only way
To stop this virus spreading
And I know you'll do what's right
For the sake of everybody.

Just keeping swimming isn't easy
You have challenges to face
But I know that you will do it
To help give hope to mankind

IF YOU WANT TO HAVE SOMETHING DIFFERENT

If you want to have something different
You can't do things the same way
Everything must be transformed
To create the changes necessary

And this precious time is now
When the world is all on pause
We all have to be at home
Nobody can go anywhere

Life will never be the same
We need to face this fact
And begin to create anew
For the life that is to come

I know I'm doing something
I swore that I'd never do
Teaching never was my choice
Especially not my children!

And if I care to bet on you
Things are different for you
Your life has been transformed as mine
We're starting our new world

How will you be a part of it?
Where will you make that difference?
I know I never thought I'd write
The way I have been doing

And you too can live this life
Making the world brand new
Your contribution changing things
The way that you can do it

You really are unique you know?
Your life can make a difference
Nobody can do what you can do
Or in the way you do it

I'd love to see what you can do
The changes you can make
The new existence that you bring
For generations to come

Making that change could be the chance
That transforms the life of others
Just because you may not know that
Doesn't mean you can't do it.

WHAT PRESENT WILL YOU UNWRAP

What present will you unwrap
On the day you step into freedom?
When your life has been returned to you
And the feeling of relief is so strong

Relief that your life can "return again"
It will never be the same
As the one you had before
Because that was then and this is now

Will you have been diligent?
Preparing for your brand-new life
It's not as easy as it sounds
But I know that you can do it

Sometimes it is easier to start
And move in the brave new world
Or you could stay stuck forever
Mourning your old way of life

This brave new world of ours can be
The best there ever was
You can begin anew, my friend
And I would urge you to try

So come on down here with me
Begin to plan what freedom means
Prepare your life for what may come
You have the power to do it

No longer would your dreams be dreams
You can make them reality
We have the time to get ready
Let us use it beautifully

Come along and plan for it
I know you are ready
There are things to change right now
That only you can do

DO YOU HAVE THE COURAGE?

Do you have the courage to be the change?
In a world full of darkness where nobody listens
Will you be the one to make that difference
And the answer to their wishes?

It's not always easy to be that one
Sometimes you will stand alone
Waiting for others to join you
Stepping out into the truth

They lie in wait to hear your voice
To find the answers that they need
You are the one to heal the differences
And bring them to that world of light

Do you have the courage for this?
Can you be the one people come to?
Will you sometimes stand alone?
And be brave when that moment comes?

I'm not saying this is simple
I'm not denying the truth in life
To make that difference you must stand
And be confident in what you say

You really can bring that life
And hope to those in need
Your richest toil ever completed
And faith in what's to be

I pray you will always be that one
No one can compare with you
Every one is different
But we can all help each other heal

THOSE OF US WHO'VE STAYED INDOORS

Those of us who've stayed indoors
Haven't always found it easy
It's not what we want deep inside
But is what we have had to do

Going out is much more fun
And seeing other people
But we know it's right to stay inside
And not be with the friends we love

I pray all will be well with you
And with your loved ones too
This isn't how we thought life would be
A year ago is a world away!

The silence of the streets abound,
As people stay where they should be
It makes you notice other things
Like the love you share with others

Our life is one brief moment
In history, then we're gone
But we can make a difference
By doing the right thing right now

Generations will look back
And wonder what it was like
They won't have any concept
Of the world we left behind

That life just seems so far away
And will never come back again
The new world on the other side
Will be just what we make it

So we need to plan indoors
Our new life waiting for us
It will be different, that we know
But how will we prepare for it?

I WONDER

I wonder at the poetry I'm creating now
A standard I never thought I could attain
There are so many words and phrases
Coming quickly to my mind

I wonder at the world around me
And the things that we are going through
The whole world is in lockdown
To preserve the life of many

I know that it's not popular
To live a life shut away
But this is the way to fight this disease
Everyone must join the battle

It's not an army that they're raising
And nobody's going "out" to war
"We're staying at home!" is the new war cry
People fight with brushes and soap

So what shall we do in these days then?
Just sit around and mope?
No, we must be strong for others
And everyone stay safe indoors

Everyone but the key workers
They must face life on the outside
Putting their lives on the line for us
So that we can be healthy and strong.

I WAS THINKING OF A TREE

I was thinking of a tree
That had survived many years
And knew it was prepared
For many more to come

It wasn't one that was protected
By other trees surrounding it
It had grown strong in wind and gale
Proudly setting roots firm in the soil

There were years it had been bent
And torn and twisted by the wind
But that didn't matter to the tree
Where it was in the ground

So we can take the tree away
And impose ourselves instead.
We can just let the changes happen
Or we can decide to use them

We haven't uncovered the best yet
Of what this new world will be
There are many differences to come
In the shape of our new society

So how do we prepare then?
By working out the changes we want
And deciding on how to set about them
When we are free to go out again

THINGS THEY SAID COULD NEVER BE DONE

Things they said could never be done
Are found out not to be so
As the whole world is isolating
People are discovering what can be

This is a time the whole world is changing
And you can be part of it too
Look all around with brand new eyes
Find the differences that can be made

Such an important thing to do
To be useful in the new world
Creating something in your mind
And bringing it forth to the world

How will you live in the new world?
Well only you can really say
It's not going to be an easy time
But we can create things if we try

So many things could be so different
And I don't know all of them
But your life is different to mine
We now have the time to find them

Focus on these beautiful changes
And find what really can be done
Create the differences you want
And bring them out into the light

A NEW WORLD IS EMERGING

A new world is emerging,
Not like the one we had before.
How do you think things can change?
To make life for new generations?

A new life will be facing them
Not like they had before
Will you be part of the change
Or hold on to what you had?

Our lives won't be the same
We can't hold on to the past
Now is the time for us to pause
Think how things can be different

Yes a change is never pleasant
And birth always comes with pain
And we are pregnantly holding
The life that is to come

Giving birth is such a mixture
Of pleasure and of pain
And we now have time to prepare
For all that there is going to be

Of course there will be some surprises
Things we haven't planned for
But the time we spent preparing
Will no doubt help us deal with them

CREATION

Creation comes in many forms
And different ways to all
Nobody thinks the same way
Everybody is totally unique

Maybe they might look different
Possibly say the same thing
But each creator has their flair
That nobody else can copy

You might want the world to stay the same
But everything is changing
It will never be the same
When we emerge from our cocoons

You can be part of this new life
And start to make a difference
Plan things out within your mind
Change how you create your world

It may look just the same to all
But you know the transformation
That you now have put in place
Making your heart grateful

So many things to consider
At the start of something new
But I know that we can do it
If only we put our minds to it

BE KIND

In these days of solitude
One thing must be remembered
Because it's so important
And that's kindness to all

The moments when you want to snap
Just pause a second and think
"They are struggling just like me
So I must always be kind."

Kind through the darkest days
Especially the darkest nights
When you wonder why and what next?
The times you want to cry and scream

A whisper can come to you
Remember what I said
Kindness can be your shield
Bringing happiness to all

Being kind is being thoughtful
Remember what we're facing
This has never been before
With the world all locked down

We've discovered what's important
And who's important too
The people that surround us
And bring us joy and love

WHAT WILL YOU BE DOING?

What will you be doing
In the days that lie ahead?
A chance to transform yourself
Into what you're meant to be

Will you paint your life anew?
Sweeping the canvas clean again
You can create a new world too
And revel in its beauty

What do you need in this time of crisis?
Where are you going to find it?
Staying home just doesn't seem right
Although we have to do it

Finding answers that we seek
Is not the easiest thing to do
You shouldn't have to go outdoors
Your life is built around them

It's scary when you take each step
Never a waste of your time
But you discover glorious things
When you take the chance

WHAT WILL YOU NEED TO LEAVE BEHIND?

What will you need to leave behind
The day we march into our new lives?
Do we want expectations from our past
To follow us into the future?

We must believe that our lives
Won't be the same again
Something has come in between
Our new existence has begun

Did you want to do new things?
Something you thought you could never do
There are open doors ahead
Just try them and then you'll see

In this strange half-life we're living
We find we can do new things
So prepare for what you want to do
Your new life is awaiting you

There is time to sit and think
And work out your new way of being
But while we do this do not forget
The things that we must leave behind

You can discard the old life now
And plan for something different
Nothing will be the same again
Because everything will change

Things might look the same as ever
But what we bring is not
It will not be the same
And that's what makes it different

IT'S IN THAT MOMENT OF WAITING

It's in that moment of waiting
The agonising suspense that surrounds you
People find out who they really are
And what they would love to be

You can't really describe that time
As emotions run far and wide
Drinking up each heartbeat
Echoing that picture outside

Is there a stab of disappointment
Or a glorious one of hope?
You know now that things can change
Yet see it there in front of you

What do you say in that time
That time from the past to the present?
There's an amazing new world to explore
A present unopened before you

Yet other times are meaningless
Just day and day after dreary day
What are you going to do about this
To change the way things are?

There's a world of possibility
A mountain top to climb
And yet you stand there waiting
As we pause that moment in time

I love to see opportunity
Just how some things could change
But what are you going to do about it?
Your vision can now be exposed

In that moment of waiting
Prepare for what lies ahead
Be ready for situations to change
It's going to be quite a journey

ALL THE WORLD

All the world is in seclusion
A silent assassin walks the streets
He cannot be traced for he's stealthy
Looking for those he can kill

Our best choice is to stay inside
And keep still while he's defeated
But it's not an easy answer
As people long for the outdoors

So what can we do in these times
When the answer is stay still?
We cannot solve this mystery
While the bug is waiting to kill

The world is held in waiting
While the virus goes on and spreads
A chance to mourn the old life
While preparing for what lies ahead

We know that it will be different
As the old life cannot remain
How it is different is up to us
As we prepare for the future

So let's get together and plan
The new life in front of us
Yes, everything will be different
But we can make a plan online

Or paper if it's easier
Anywhere in fact
It doesn't matter where we plan
Our future lies before us

So come on to the future my friend
It's waiting for us all
A chance to change everything
And make our lives anew

THE WHOLE WORLD IS UNDER TRIAL

The whole world is under trial
But what will it bring forth?
Will you be found wanting
For the meaning for your life?

What will people be looking for
When this time is over?
Will they find some relief
In spending time with others?

If you're on a voyage of discovery
This could be a great bonding time
Where you find out secret things
People around have been holding back so long.

But when the trial is over
You will find what you've become
The changes it has brought in you
And the meaning of your life

It's not an easy situation we are in
But is what we are facing
We need to carry on with life
Even though we are home

The trial is not yet over
Everything chops and changes
As the situation carries on
We must choose what to do

Things are quite bad right now
But we know they will improve
As long as we are careful
We can protect those around us

WAITING, WAITING FOR RELEASE

Waiting, waiting for release
Every one of us does it
There must be a reason for it
It's a thing that we all do

It's important to realise
The reason we all do it
The waiting can be short or long
Impacting our daily lives

Sometimes people know you're waiting
At other times they don't
It doesn't really matter which
It's the waiting that's important

There are times of anticipation
Where others can wait with you
Waiting doesn't ask permission
It imposes itself on you

When time is over the release
Is such a great relief
Your life has changed forever
Into something new

It may just be a tiny change
Or it could be massive one
There could be a rainbow
On the other side of it all

So please don't be impatient
Just wait for the right time
When release is given to you
A joy from all the waiting

LOVE IS FOUND

Love is found within the heart
By you or someone else
It doesn't really matter who
It needs to be discovered

There are some artworks I admire
Appreciate the creativity in them
And other pieces that I LOVE
Would be happy to display at home

Love is not called to be silent
She may whisper a loving cheer
Or she could yell out with excitement
At things you have achieved

But most of all she offers comfort
To a poor soul needing solace
Consolation for whatever
Has led them to this place

And love always comes back to you
The dove, returned again
Wanting to find a place of rest
Returning to ease your soul

CAN YOU TRUST

Can you trust things will be alright?
Even though it doesn't feel it?
We've never weathered this before
Well, you have to now

What will my new life be like?
Well, that you have to compose
All our lives look very different
Because we're all individuals

You think your life isn't what it was
Well, it won't ever be that again
You may miss what has been
The chance now is a new life

With each new challenge you'll be stronger Determination
will see you through
But can you trust things will be great?
Even though you can't find the way?

It will be fine, I promise you this
Whichever side of eternity you sit
Everything will turn out right
Although you might not see it

RETURNING

Returning back to life isn't easy
Although it may look simple
Taking stock of your emotions
Really isn't factored in

Yes you can go back to work
Because that's what you do
But nothing is the same
Your emotions are so different

It's not like it used to be
No, it never can be
We are a complexity
With how we react to things

Individuality may have changed
And return as something else
People are not the same
Nor will their response be

So remember to be gentle to all
And include in that yourself
You need to make exceptions
For those who find it hard

Everybody needs some grace
Especially the children
They have got big feelings too
While living this new life

Something they will never forget
The days the schools shut down
Leaving them in the darkness
Of a life lived in isolation

NORMAL

People want life to go back to normal
But normal it never was
It may look like some other people's
But it has to become a new reality

Many things will seem as usual
But normal doesn't really exist
When your life has been interrupted
There is a before and after

Life has always been divided into
What was and what will be
A massive jolt forever changes things
Like an electric shock

There has not been something similar
For over one hundred years
No information we can draw from
Telling us what to do

This has been so unprecedented
People not knowing to do
Living their lives as though in isolation
Yet still wanting others

We will never forget these years that passed
Troubling us indeed
These memories will remain alive
As long as we live

But our new life will be different
Although forever changed
We are what we always were
And will continue to be

AUTHOR'S FAREWELL

I am going to say Goodbye now
It's time for me to finish
So many poems written to help
Others in their need

There are so many things to do now
I must get on and finish
It was a pleasure walking with you
And spending time with you

Sometimes you need that treasure
Of walking with someone else
You can travel along together
Along a path barely worn

We are separate individuals
Going along a path together
But it's time now for me to end
My journey doesn't stop here

You'll see me again soon, I promise
We can be together again
All you have to do is find me
And enjoy what my poems bring

I'd love to see you again someday
That would be really great
If you love the poems I wrote
Please share them with another.

Thank you for reading my work
I hope that it has touched you
Deep inside within your being
And made a change within you

ACKNOWLEDGMENTS

I would first of all like to acknowledge my friend Sheila who encouraged me to write poems in my late teens and twenties and even got me to send some of them into competitions. I also want to mention my dear husband, who would find me writing poetry at late evening because I had just got inspired by a word, a look, a touch,or read and I would be up writing and correcting for hours. I would also like to thank the people who read these poems for me and corrected the mistakes in them. There's many of you and I am grateful for you all. I also want to thank the people that were there for me and supported and helped me in my effort to make this into a poetry book. I am truly grateful to you all and could never repay you for your kindness and support.

ABOUT THE AUTHOR

Anika writes from her adopted country of Scotland, where she lives with her husband, their son, two cats and a dog. Anika has been writing poems since her late teens and early twenties, when she was encouraged by a friend to submit some of her work to poetry competitions. You can find more information on her website at www.anikaspeaks.com

Printed in Great Britain
by Amazon

69144087R00058